GW00503815

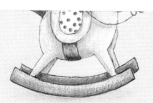

This book is a celebration
of a life that's just begun,
so congratulations now that you have
your brand new little one !

It's so good to hear your news,
your future's looking bright
and it is so very wonderful
to share in your delight.

Your days of expectation
are suddenly in the past,
for your beautiful baby girl
is now with you at last.

What better reason
can there be
to have a celebration
than when you
welcome to the world
a brand new generation !

This sweet ray of sunshine
will light up all your days
and your life has changed forever
in the very best of ways.

She is so cute and cuddly
and sets your heart awhirl.
She brightens every single day
- your own little baby girl !

She's a special delivery
who's labelled with love,
wrapped by an angel
and sent from above !

A baby girl so small and soft,
her skin feels just like cream,
she's sweet as sugared candyfloss
and pretty as a dream.

From her small downy head
to her two tiny feet,
she is the perfect package,
so lovely and complete.

You look at her angelic face
and tiny chubby limbs,
you offer out your finger
to a little hand that clings.

She has ten little fingers,
ten curled up toes,
the softest silky skin
and the cutest button nose.

Eyes that stare with innocence
at the big world all around,
those funny little gurgles
and strange contented sounds.

There is nothing to compare
with her enchanting gaze,
her giggles of delight
and all her lovely ways.

A brand new baby girl
is perfection pure and simple,
in each tiny feature
and every little dimple.

This perfect little person
who chuckles happily
will become the main attraction
with friends and family.

She's cute and sweet and wonderful,
she's all these things and more.
She's your own little baby girl
to care for and adore !

Along with all the good bits
there will be challenges for you
and it may be slightly daunting,
when it's all so very new.

You'll have sleepless nights,
constant feeding,
smelly nappies too,
as well as endless washing
and other baby things to do !

At first there may be chaos
and things will get left undone,
but all that really matters
is your gorgeous little one.

You'll become a natural
if you take things day by day,
plus there'll be lots of people
who will help along the way.

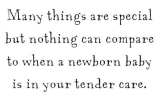

Many things are special
but nothing can compare
to when a newborn baby
is in your tender care.

As you watch her sleeping
you can't believe it's true,
that this little person lying there
really is a part of you!

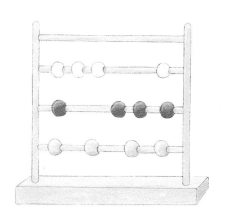

So many new experiences
are about to come your way
and you have the thrill of watching her
as she grows and learns each day.

Her first words and favourite toys,
her special little ways
will all add to the happiness
of precious baby days.

Her future's surely rosy
as long as you're around
to nurture and support her
and keep her feet on the ground.

You're sure to love your little one,
you'll be so protective too,
and she is also bound to give
the same love back to you.

Her big eyes look up at you
as she gurgles happily
and how very proud she's made you
is plain for all to see.

She hasn't been here very long
but already you're so sure
that no other parent on this earth
could love their daughter more.

It is so very special
the love you feel for her today
– this feeling's very powerful
and will never fade away.

The bond will grow between you,
so loving and so strong.
It's one that can't be broken
and will last your whole lives long.

You'll always be there for her
through all the smiles and tears
to give her so much love
that will last throughout the years.

There'll be kisses by the dozen,
cuddles by the score
and a tender loving feeling
that you'll know forever more.

She'll fill your life with happiness
as that's what babies do
and the world will be her oyster
all because of you !

She'll twist you round her finger,
turn your whole world inside out,
you'll melt just at the sight of her,
that's what daughters are all about !

So it's hoped the future brings you
everything you want it to
and may each day be happy
for your baby and for you.